T0402878

Momentous Materials

Graphene

by Dalton Rains

FOCUS READERS.

BEACON

www.focusreaders.com

Copyright © 2024 by Focus Readers®, Mendota Heights, MN 55120. All rights reserved. No part of this book may be reproduced or utilized in any form or by any means without written permission from the publisher.

Focus Readers is distributed by North Star Editions: sales@northstareditions.com | 888-417-0195

Produced for Focus Readers by Red Line Editorial.

Photographs ©: iStockphoto, cover, 1; James Atoa/UPI/Alamy Live News/Alamy, 4; Shutterstock Images, 7, 8, 10, 20, 22, 25, 27, 29; Joe Buglewicz/AP Images, 13; Colin McPherson/Corbis News/Getty Images, 14–15; Hufton+Crow-VIEW/Alamy, 16; Kirill Kukhmar/TASS/Newscom, 18

Library of Congress Cataloging-in-Publication Data
Names: Rains, Dalton, author.
Title: Graphene / by Dalton Rains.
Description: Mendota Heights, MN : Focus Readers, [2024] | Series: Momentous materials | Includes bibliographical references and index. | Audience: Grades 2-3
Identifiers: LCCN 2023033126 (print) | LCCN 2023033127 (ebook) | ISBN 9798889980339 (hardcover) | ISBN 9798889980766 (paperback) | ISBN 9798889981589 (ebook pdf) | ISBN 9798889981190 (hosted ebook)
Subjects: LCSH: Graphene--Juvenile literature. | Graphite--Juvenile literature.
Classification: LCC TA455.G65 R35 2024 (print) | LCC TA455.G65 (ebook) | DDC 662/.92--dc23/eng/20230731
LC record available at https://lccn.loc.gov/2023033126
LC ebook record available at https://lccn.loc.gov/2023033127

Printed in the United States of America
Mankato, MN
012024

About the Author

Dalton Rains is a writer and editor from Saint Paul, Minnesota.

Table of Contents

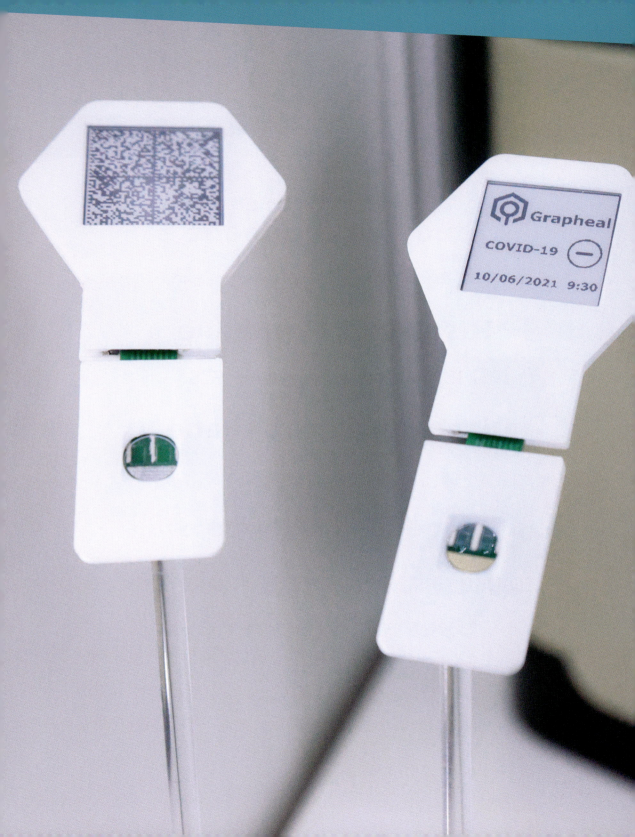

Chapter 1

Studying Graphene

A **lab** is filled with scientists. They are studying graphene. This material is very thin. And it has many uses. Some scientists want to use graphene in medicine.

Graphene blood tests can help find diseases very quickly.

They study ways that it can be used to make blood tests.

Other scientists want to use graphene to deliver drugs. The material can help move medicine through people's bodies.

In a different lab, scientists focus on sports equipment. Some are trying to create better shoes.

Did You Know?

Three million layers of graphene would be thinner than a penny.

 In the 2010s, a company started selling motorcycle helmets made with graphene.

Graphene could make them last longer. Other scientists are working on helmets. Graphene could make them extra strong.

Chapter 2

History of Graphene

Graphene is not found in nature. But graphite is. Graphite is a soft **mineral**. For hundreds of years, people have used it to write. In 1859, a scientist made a discovery.

Graphite was first used to make pencils in the late 1700s.

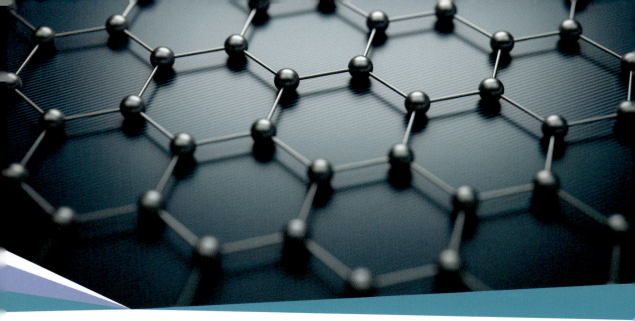

 The hexagon shape of carbon atoms is what makes graphene so strong.

He realized graphite was made up of many layers of **carbon**.

In the 1900s, more scientists became interested in graphite. They studied thin flakes of it. Scientists **theorized** a new material. It was a single layer of carbon **atoms**.

They thought the atoms would be arranged in hexagons. Those shapes would join together like a honeycomb. Scientists called the material graphene. But for many years, they couldn't figure out how to make it.

Scientists made graphene for the first time in 2004. The material had many useful properties. It was strong. Also, electricity flowed through it easily. Soon, scientists made the first graphene transistor.

Transistors are small parts that help computers work.

By the early 2010s, some companies sold products that used graphene. Scientists also invented new products. In 2015, they made a graphene filter. It could remove salt from seawater. Scientists hoped

Did You Know?

The scientists who created graphene won the Nobel Prize for their work. That is the biggest award in science.

 Graphene batteries can stand up to high temperatures. Other batteries cannot.

it could help more people get fresh water.

In 2018, scientists found another way to use graphene. They made a device that stored electricity. It charged much faster than other kinds of batteries.

Discovering Graphene

Graphene was discovered by two scientists in the United Kingdom. One day, they put sticky tape on piece of graphite. When they pulled it off, thin flakes stuck to the tape. They used tape to split the flakes again and again. After doing this many times, they could dissolve the tape. That left behind very thin pieces from the graphite. The scientists looked at these pieces under a **microscope**. They had made graphene for the first time.

Andre Geim led the team of scientists who first made graphene.

Chapter 3

Modern Methods

Scientists make graphene in different ways. One method is similar to how graphene was discovered. It starts with graphite. Scientists use **adhesives** to pull away thin flakes of graphene.

 A lab in England specializes in making graphene.

 A scientist produces graphene at a lab in Russia.

However, it's difficult to make large amounts of graphene in this way.

Other methods let scientists grow graphene. First, they put gas in a chamber. The chamber has a heated surface. Gas atoms come together. They form a thin layer on the surface of the chamber. Then, scientists release the rest of the gas. Graphene is left behind. This process requires expensive equipment. But it helps scientists make high-quality graphene.

Did You Know?

A sheet of graphene the size of a football field would weigh less than a paper clip.

 Many scientists work at the National Graphene Institute in Manchester, England.

A different method lets scientists make larger amounts of graphene. They add oxygen to graphite. Then they mix it with liquid. That causes a kind of graphene to form.

Scientists can make large amounts of this graphene. However, it is less pure. The method can break the hexagon shapes of the graphene. That can create holes in the material. As a result, the graphene is weaker. Even so, scientists have found uses for this lower-quality graphene.

None of these methods are perfect. So, scientists continue working. They hope to find new ways of creating graphene.

Chapter 4

Uses of Graphene

By the early 2020s, only a few companies sold graphene. Scientists were still learning how to make large amounts. But they were excited to use it for different things.

 Some people put graphene coatings on their cars to protect them from dirt and water.

Scientists hoped to use graphene to make products stronger and lighter. For example, graphene could be added to vehicles. These could include cars, bikes, and airplanes. Graphene could help them go faster. It could also help them use less energy. The material could protect people, too.

Did You Know?

Graphene is 200 times stronger than steel.

 Some sports cars are made with graphene to make them faster and safer.

Scientists also hoped to use graphene in electronics. The material could help make computers more powerful. That's because it can be used to make faster transistors. Graphene could also help cool down electronics.

The material may have other uses, too. For example, scientists were working on making flexible screens. The screens could let phones or tablets roll up like paper.

Scientists were also excited about how graphene could help the environment. It could be used to help produce **renewable energy**. Graphene has already been used to make solar panels. But scientists hoped to improve this technology. Graphene may even be used to

 Graphene solar panels are an Earth-friendly source of electricity.

remove **pollution**. For instance, graphene filters may clean the air. This amazing material could help create a better future.

FOCUS ON
Graphene

Write your answers on a separate piece of paper.

1. Write a paragraph describing the main ideas of Chapter 3.

2. What do you think is the most interesting way graphene could be used in the future? Why?

3. What mineral did scientists use to make graphene?
- **A.** steel
- **B.** graphite
- **C.** oxygen

4. Why might only a few companies sell graphene products?
- **A.** because graphene cannot be used for many things
- **B.** because graphene is difficult and expensive to make
- **C.** because no one wants to use graphene products

5. What does the word **deliver** mean in this book?

*Other scientists want to use graphene to **deliver** drugs. The material can help move medicine through people's bodies.*

    A. to bring or send somewhere
    B. to create new kinds of something
    C. to look at something up close

6. What does the word **flexible** mean in this book?

*For example, scientists were working on making **flexible** screens. The screens could let phones or tablets roll up like paper.*

    A. very stiff
    B. able to bend
    C. quick or fast

Answer key on page 32.

Glossary

adhesives
Materials that make objects stick together.

atoms
Small units of matter that the objects around us are made of.

carbon
One of the basic chemical elements of all living things.

lab
A room or building where scientists do experiments.

microscope
A tool that makes very small things look bigger.

mineral
A substance that forms naturally under the ground.

pollution
Harmful substances that collect in the air, water, or soil.

renewable energy
Energy produced from a source that will not run out.

theorized
Made a guess about how something works.

To Learn More

BOOKS

Kim, Carol. *Hidden Heroes in Technology*. Minneapolis: Lerner Publications, 2023.

Lewis, Carrie. *My House in 2055*. Minneapolis: Lerner Publications, 2021.

Pettiford, Rebecca. *Computers*. Minneapolis: Bellwether Media, 2022.

NOTE TO EDUCATORS

Visit **www.focusreaders.com** to find lesson plans, activities, links, and other resources related to this title.

Index

Answer Key: 1. Answers will vary; **2.** Answers will vary; **3.** B; **4.** B; **5.** A; **6.** B